KT-496-807

CONTENTS

ERISKAY, WESTERN ISLES 1963 E188009

Flavours of... SCOTLAND

RECIPES

Compiled by Julia Skinner

THE FRANCIS FRITH COLLECTION

www.francisfrith.com

First published in the United Kingdom in 2011 by The Francis Frith Collection®

This edition published exclusively for Bradwell Books in 2014
For trade enquiries see: www.bradwellbooks.com or tel: 0800 834 920
ISBN 978-1-84589-552-5

Text and Design copyright The Francis Frith Collection®
Photographs copyright The Francis Frith Collection® except where indicated.

The Frith® photographs and the Frith® logo are reproduced under licence from
Heritage Photographic Resources Ltd, the owners of the Frith® archive and trademarks.
'The Francis Frith Collection', 'Francis Frith' and 'Frith' are registered trademarks of
Heritage Photographic Resources Ltd.

All rights reserved. No photograph in this publication may be sold to a third party other than in the original
form of this publication, or framed for sale to a third party. No parts of this publication may be reproduced,
stored in a retrieval system, or transmitted, in any form, or by any means, electronic, mechanical, photocopying,
recording or otherwise, without the prior permission of the publishers and copyright holder.

British Library Cataloguing in Publication Data

Flavours of Scotland - Recipes
Compiled by Julia Skinner

The Francis Frith Collection
6 Oakley Business Park,
Wylye Road, Dinton,
Wiltshire SP3 5EU
Tel: +44 (0) 1722 716 376
Email: info@francisfrith.co.uk
www.francisfrith.com

Printed and bound in Malaysia
Contains material sourced from responsibly managed forests

Front Cover: **FRASERBURGH, HERRING BOATS c1900** F63002p
Frontispiece: **INVERLOCHY, THE CASTLE c1890** I3000I

The colour-tinting is for illustrative purposes only, and is not intended to be historically accurate

AS WITH ANY HISTORICAL DATABASE, THE FRANCIS FRITH ARCHIVE IS CONSTANTLY BEING
CORRECTED AND IMPROVED, AND THE PUBLISHERS WOULD WELCOME INFORMATION ON
OMISSIONS OR INACCURACIES

RECIPE

SCOTS BROTH

This filling soup, also known as Scotch Broth, or Barley Broth, would originally have been made with mutton, but nowadays is more commonly made with lamb. This broth won the approval of the notoriously hard-to-please Dr Samuel Johnson when he toured Scotland with James Boswell in 1773. 'At dinner, Dr Johnson ate several plate-fuls of Scotch broth, with barley and peas in it, and seemed very fond of the dish. I said, 'You never ate it before?'. Johnson. 'No sir; but I don't care how soon I eat it again.' ('Journal of a Tour to the Hebrides', 1786, James Boswell)

> 1kg/2 lbs lean neck of lamb, cut into small chunks
> 1.75 litres/3 pints water
> 1 large onion
> 50g/2oz pearl barley
> 75g/3oz dried peas (soaked in water overnight) or fresh peas
> 1 bouquet garni
> 1 large carrot, chopped
> 1 turnip, chopped
> 3 leeks, trimmed, thoroughly washed and chopped
> Half a small white cabbage, shredded
> Salt and pepper

Put the lamb and water into a large saucepan, bring to the boil and carefully skim off any scum which rises to the surface. Add the onion, pearl barley, peas and bouquet garni. Partly cover the saucepan, reduce the heat and simmer gently for 1 hour. Add the remaining vegetables, and season to taste. Bring back to the boil, then cover again and simmer for a further 30-40 minutes, until the vegetables are tender. Skim off any fat from the top of the soup, remove the bouquet garni and serve piping hot.

RECIPE

COCK-A-LEEKIE SOUP

This famous Scottish dish is more of a stew than a soup. It is a very old recipe, and was recorded in 1598 when Fynes Morrison described a dish he had eaten whilst dining at a knight's house in Scotland: '… but the upper messe, insteede of Porredge, had a Pullet with some prunes in the broth'. There is a story that the soup originated in the days when cockfighting was a popular sport, and the losing cock was eaten after the contest, thrown into a stock pot with some leeks. The addition of prunes for extra flavour was a later refinement, although some cooks nowadays omit these, or remove them before serving. The prunes can either be used whole, or stoned and roughly chopped if preferred.

> 1 small chicken about 1.2kg (2lbs 10oz)
> 6-8 thick leeks, trimmed, washed and roughly chopped,
>   keeping the green and white parts separate
> 6 black peppercorns
> 2 fresh bay leaves
> 12 prunes, soaked in cold water for several hours
> 2 tablespoonfuls finely chopped fresh parsley
> Salt to taste

Put the chicken in a large saucepan. Add the green parts of the leeks, the peppercorns, bay leaves and just enough water to cover the chicken. Bring slowly to the boil then reduce the heat, cover the pan with a tight-fitting lid and simmer for 20-25 minutes. Remove from the heat, keep the pan covered and leave for about 1 hour, until the chicken is cooked and tender. Remove the chicken from the pan carefully and place in a sieve over a bowl. When cool enough to handle, remove and shred the flesh, discarding the skin and bones.

Meanwhile, remove and discard the green leeks, peppercorns and bay leaves from the pan, and add the white leeks. Simmer gently until the leeks are tender, and add salt to taste. Return the chicken flesh to the pan together with the prunes, reheat gently and serve in a warm bowl, sprinkled with parsley.

RECIPE

CULLEN SKINK

Cullen Skink is a famous traditional Scottish recipe from the Moray Firth for a rich and creamy smoked haddock soup. 'Skink' comes from a Gaelic word which originally meant 'essence', but now describes a stew-like soup, whilst 'cullen' was the name for the 'seatown' (port or harbour) district of a town.

700g/1½ lbs smoked haddock (the un-dyed variety is best to use)
600ml/1 pint milk
600ml/1 pint water
2 onions, peeled – chop one onion and leave the other whole
1 blade of mace
50g/2oz butter
3 medium-sized potatoes, peeled and chopped into chunks
Salt and freshly ground black pepper
1 tablespoonful finely chopped fresh parsley
4 tablespoonfuls single cream
Chopped fresh parsley or chives, to garnish

Place the fish in a large saucepan, cover with the milk and water and add the whole onion and the mace. Bring slowly to the boil over a gentle heat, then reduce the heat and simmer very gently for 5 minutes. Remove the pan from the heat and leave to stand for 10 minutes. Strain off the cooking liquid and reserve.

In another saucepan, melt the butter, add the chopped onion and chopped potatoes and cook over a gentle heat for about 10 minutes, stirring occasionally, until the onion has started to soften. Pour the reserved, strained cooking liquid into the pan and simmer gently, until the potato pieces are soft. Remove from the heat and allow to cool slightly, then pass through a sieve or liquidize in a blender. Rinse out the saucepan, then return the liquidized soup to it.

Flake the cooked fish, being careful to remove all the bones and the skin, and stir the fish flesh into the soup. Add salt and freshly ground black pepper to taste, stir in the cream and reheat gently before serving. Serve with a garnish of finely chopped fresh parsley or chives.

RECIPE

TATTIE SOUP

This traditional soup based on 'tatties' (potatoes) is a filling and tasty way of using up old vegetables. The addition of bacon is optional, but does improve the flavour significantly. In past times, in the spring a handful of finely chopped young nettle sprigs would have been added to the soup a few minutes before serving, to add extra nutritional value, but modern cooks will probably prefer to use parsley instead.

> 450g/1 lb old potatoes
> 2 large old carrots
> 2 onions
> 4 rashers of streaky bacon with the rinds cut off (optional)
> 1.7 litres/3 pints of good stock
> Salt and freshly ground black pepper, to taste
> A handful of finely chopped fresh parsley (or nettle tops)

Peel the potatoes and cut them into very thin slices. Peel the onions and trim and scrape the carrots, and either chop them very fine, or coarsely grate them. Cut the de-rinded bacon into small pieces.

Bring the stock to the boil in a large saucepan, then add the prepared vegetables and the bacon. Reduce to simmer, cover the pan and leave to cook gently for 1½ -2 hours, until the vegetables have cooked right down and the soup has become thick. (If a smoother texture is preferred, remove the soup from the heat at this stage and allow to cool a little, then pass through a blender or liquidizer and return to the pan and heat through again.) Season to taste, and add the chopped parsley (or nettles, to be really authentic!) just before serving.

PERTH, HIGH STREET EAST 1899 43899a

SCOTTISH FISH

Scottish fish, whether caught from the sea, the lochs, or the fast-running streams and rivers, is superb. For centuries the Scots have been masters of the art of smoking fish, and the smoked salmon, haddock, kippers and bloaters produced in Scotland are unsurpassed. Herrings, known to fishermen as 'the silver darlings', are very nutritious and were a staple part of the diet in the past. They were an important catch for Scottish fishermen in the 19th and early 20th centuries, and as the herring fleet increased, gutting and curing houses sprang up in the ports of Scotland and north-east England. The herring industry was strictly seasonal, which led to major migrations of labour from port to port; the fishing harbours would be thronged with men and women working to meet the sailing schedules. Gutting and packing the fish was done by women. This was a skilled job, and a good herring woman could gut 40 fish a minute. As the women were on piece-rate it was essential to keep their fingers nimble, which they did by continuously knitting in their free time.

FRASERBURGH, THE HERRING FLEET c1900 F63002

RECIPE

HERRINGS IN OATMEAL

There would be as much activity on shore as on the boats themselves in Scotland's fishing towns and villages in the past. The Scottish fishwives and their children were kept busy collecting mussels for bait, mending nets, and knitting jerseys. Often the fishwives (such as the bonny lady seen in the photograph on page 13) had to do the job of selling the fish as well, and when landings were late owing to bad weather, they were obliged to haul the laden baskets of fish several miles to the markets to negotiate with wholesalers.

This is a popular and traditional way of eating herrings in Scotland, frying them in an oatmeal coating which goes crispy when they are cooked.

> 4 herrings
> 2 tablespoonfuls oatmeal
> Half a teaspoonful salt
> Pepper
> Fat for frying

Scale and clean the herrings and wash and dry them well. Mix the oatmeal with the salt and pepper and use this to coat the herrings on both sides, pressing the oatmeal well into the herrings.

Fry the herrings in hot fat for 5 minutes each side. The herrings can also be grilled if preferred, prepared in the same way, but frying gives them more flavour.

RECIPE

FINNAN PANCAKES

Smoking fish is one of the oldest ways of preserving food. In ancient and medieval times the Scottish smokehouses used oak and other woods to create dark-smoked haddock such as the famous Arbroath smokies that are still produced in Scotland. In the 19th century a milder, delicately smoked whole fish, the Finnan haddock (known as 'haddie'), became popular. It originated from the village of Findon, south of Aberdeen, where it was dry-salted and smoked over peat for some 8 hours. Try to buy naturally smoked fish for this recipe, without the bright yellow dye.

> 1 egg, beaten
> 175g/6oz plain flour
> 900ml/1½ pints milk
> 75g/3oz butter
> 225g/8oz smoked Finnan haddock
> Salt and pepper
> 2 eggs, hard-boiled and chopped into pieces
> 1 dessertspoonful finely chopped fresh parsley

Place 115g (4oz) of the flour in a bowl and stir in the beaten egg. Gradually blend in 300ml (½ pint) of the milk to form a smooth batter. Take 25g (1oz) of the butter to cook the pancakes. Melt a little of the butter in a frying pan, then pour in sufficient batter to thinly coat the bottom of the pan. Brown on one side, then turn the pancake and brown the other side. Remove the pancake from the pan and keep to one side. Use the batter to make more pancakes – this amount should make about 8.

Pre-heat the oven to 190°C/375°F/Gas Mark 5. Cook the smoked haddock very gently in 300ml (½ pint) of the milk until it is tender. Lift out the cooked fish with a slotted spoon and drain, reserving the cooking liquid. Break up the fish into small flakes, being sure to remove and discard any bones. Make up the liquor the fish was cooked in to 600ml (1 pint) with the remaining cold milk. Melt the remaining 50g (2oz) of butter in a saucepan, stir in the remaining flour and cook gently for 2-3 minutes, stirring occasionally. Gradually add the liquid, stirring continually so that no lumps are formed. Bring to the boil, stirring, until the mixture thickens, then reduce the heat and cook gently for a few minutes. Mix half the sauce with the flaked fish, and season to taste. Divide the filling between the pancakes, then roll up the pancakes and arrange them in a wide, greased ovenproof dish. Stir the chopped hard-boiled eggs into the remaining sauce, season to taste, then spread the sauce over the stuffed pancakes. Bake in the pre-heated oven for 15-20 minutes. Serve sprinkled with chopped fresh parsley.

**COLDINGHAM
A SCOTTISH FISHWIFE
c1932** C358024

LOCH ACHRAY, THE TROSSACHS CHURCH 1871 L89001

RECIPE

SCOTTISH SALMON WITH DILL BUTTER

Scotland's salmon and trout rivers are world-famous. The Tay, the Dee, the Spey, the Tweed and many others are all well-stocked with salmon, sea-trout and brown trout. Salmon from the River Clyde were once so important to Glasgow that the fish were incorporated into the city's coat of arms, and were so plentiful in the 17th century that servants in Glasgow stipulated that they should not be forced to eat salmon more than twice a week! In Scotland, salmon fishing is not just a sport for anglers but an important commercial livelihood for fishermen on both the east and west coasts. Scottish salmon, whether fresh or smoked, is unsurpassed.

> 4 salmon steaks
> 50g/2oz butter, softened to room temperature
> Finely grated rind of half a lemon
> 1 tablespoonful lemon juice
> 1 tablespoonful finely chopped fresh dill
> 2 lemon slices, cut into halves
> 4 sprigs of fresh dill
> Salt and freshly ground black pepper, to taste

Place the butter, lemon rind, lemon juice, chopped dill and salt and pepper in a bowl, and mix it well together with a fork, to make the dill butter. Spoon the butter mixture on to a piece of greaseproof paper and roll it up to form a sausage shape. Twist the ends together, wrap in cling film and place in the freezer or ice box of the fridge for 20 minutes, until it is firm.

Pre-heat the oven to 190°C/375°F/Gas Mark 5. Cut out four pieces of foil each big enough to encase a salmon steak, grease them lightly and place a salmon steak in the centre of each piece of foil. Remove the butter from the freezer, unwrap and slice it into 8 rounds. Place two rounds of the dill butter on top of each salmon steak with one of the lemon pieces between them, and place a sprig of dill on top. Bring up the edges of the foil to encase each piece of salmon in a foil parcel and crinkle the edges to seal firmly. Place the salmon parcels on a baking sheet and cook in the pre-heated oven for 20-25 minutes. Remove from the oven, undo the foil and slide the salmon steaks with their topping on to warmed serving plates, pour the juices from the parcel on to each salmon steak and serve.

RECIPE

SCOTTISH SMOKED SALMON, CUCUMBER AND HERB TART

Scotland has a long tradition of smoking both haddock and salmon of excellent quality. This makes an unusual and tasty savoury tart, ideal for a summer's day lunch or a picnic.

> 225g/8oz shortcrust pastry
> A little beaten egg for the pastry base
> 1 large cucumber, skinned and chopped into small chunks
> Salt and freshly ground black pepper
> 225g/8oz smoked salmon, broken into good-sized pieces
> 225g/8oz cream cheese, or soft cheese such as Philadelphia
> 2 eggs, plus 1 extra egg yolk
> 150ml/ ¼ pint double cream
> 2 tablespoonfuls finely chopped fresh parsley
> 2 tablespoonfuls finely chopped fresh chives
> 2 tablespoonfuls finely chopped fresh dill
> Finely grated zest of 1 lemon
> Juice of 1 lemon

Pre-heat the oven to 200ºC/400ºF/Gas Mark 6. Roll out the pastry on a lightly floured surface, and use it to line a large, shallow, greased tart or flan tin or dish. Place a piece of greaseproof paper with some baking beans on the pastry base, and bake blind in the pre-heated oven for 15 minutes. Remove from the oven and take out the greaseproof paper and baking beans. Prick the pastry base all over with a fork, brush the pastry case all over with beaten egg to seal it, and return to the oven for a further 5-10 minutes, until the pastry base has turned a light golden brown.

Put the chopped pieces of cucumber in a colander and sprinkle lightly with salt. Cover the cucumber with a small plate and put a heavy object on top of the plate – this helps to force out some of the liquid from the cucumber. Place the colander in a bowl or in the sink and leave for 30 minutes, by which time some of the cucumber liquid will have drained away. Rinse the cucumber, then drain and dry in kitchen paper. Arrange the cucumber pieces with the smoked salmon in the pre-baked pastry case. Put the cream cheese or soft cheese, eggs, egg yolk, cream, herbs, lemon zest and lemon juice into a bowl with salt and pepper to taste and beat or whisk together until well mixed. Spoon the cheese mixture over the salmon and cucumber in the pastry case. Bake in the oven at 200°C/400°F/Gas Mark 6 for 30 minutes, or until the tart is cooked but not dry, and the filling is risen and firm to the touch. This can be eaten warm or cold.

LOCH LUBNAIG 1899 44428

ISLE OF SKYE, OLD HOUSE NEAR LOCH CAIRIDH 1962 S427011

Flavours of ...
SCOTLAND
MEAT, POULTRY & GAME

RECIPE

ABERDEEN ANGUS STEAKS WITH WHISKY SAUCE

Scotland produces some of the best meat in the world, including tender lamb and well-flavoured mutton from sheep that have grazed on heather, and succulent beef from the Aberdeen Angus breed of cattle that was developed in the north-east of Scotland in the early 19th century. This is a luxury recipe for a special occasion, using the finest Scottish beef steaks with an indulgent whisky sauce. This quantity serves 4 – if you are only cooking for two, halve the quantities for the sauce.

> 115g/4oz butter
> 1 onion, peeled and finely chopped
> 4 Aberdeen Angus fillet steaks, about 175g (6oz) each in weight
> Salt and freshly ground black pepper
> 4 tablespoonfuls of whisky
> 115g/4oz mushrooms, thinly sliced
> 1 teaspoonful coarse-grain mustard
> 300ml/ ½ pint beef stock
> 150ml/ ¼ pint cream

Melt the butter in a frying pan and gently sauté the finely chopped onion until it is soft and transparent, then increase the heat and add the steaks. Cook the steaks for 3-5 minutes on each side depending on their thickness and individual preference. Remove the steaks to a hot dish and keep warm whilst the sauce is prepared.

Drain off the excess fat from the pan and add the whisky. Use a wooden spoon to stir up the residue from the bottom of the pan and mix in all the juices. Add the stock, mustard and sliced mushrooms. Increase the heat to boil the sauce and reduce it to a thick syrup. Reduce the heat, add the cream and heat through gently. Season the sauce to taste, then pour it over the steaks and serve immediately.

RECIPE

SCOTS COLLOPS

'Collop' is an old word for a slice of meat. A dish of collops of venison, beef or lamb is traditionally served in Scotland on Burns' Night, 25th January (see opposite). This recipe uses collops of fine Scottish beef.

> 4 onions, peeled and sliced
> 115g/4oz mushrooms, finely chopped
> 50g/2oz butter
> 1 tablespoonful oil, for frying
> 4 thin slices of Scottish rump steak
>   – about 1cm (½ inch) thick
> Salt and pepper

Heat the butter and oil together in a large frying pan and fry the onions until they are well-browned and cooked through. Remove them to a hot dish and keep warm.

Increase the heat and fry the steak slices in the remaining fat in the pan, allowing 2-3 minutes on each side, then add the steaks to the dish with the onions, stir them around a little with the onions and season to taste with salt and pepper. Keep warm whilst you cook the mushrooms.

Add the mushrooms to the frying pan, season to taste and cook gently until their juices are running a little. Tip out the mushrooms and the cooking juices on top of the steaks, and serve immediately.

HAGGIS AND ROBERT BURNS

Fair fa' your honest sonsie face
Great chieftain o' the puddin' race!
(From 'To a Haggis', Robert Burns)

Robert (Rabbie) Burns is thought by many to be Scotland's greatest poet. He was born in a simple cottage in the village of Alloway on 25th January 1759 and died in Dumfries in 1796 at the early age of thirty-seven. His birthplace at Alloway, a 'but and ben', or two-room clay cottage, was built by the poet's father, and later became an inn. In 1881 the cottage was purchased by the trustees of the Burns Monument and opened as a museum. Alloway is now the centre of pilgrimage for lovers of Burns's poetry.

The life and works of Robert Burns are celebrated in Scotland each year on Burns' Night, 25th January, with a special Burns' Night Supper. Much merrymaking takes place, special toasts are drunk and traditional dishes are eaten – especially Scotland's most famous dish, haggis. Haggis is rather like a large, oval-shaped sausage, made from a sheep's stomach stuffed with oatmeal and the minced or chopped parts of an animal which might otherwise be discarded, such as the heart, lungs and liver (the finest haggis uses liver from a deer, rather than a sheep). Haggis is traditionally served with Bashed Neeps - see page 30. At Burns' Night celebrations the haggis is brought in to the accompaniment of a piper, and placed ceremoniously before the chief guest. 'To a Haggis' by Robert Burns is then recited, and the haggis is toasted with drams of whisky before being eaten.

Queen Victoria was served haggis whilst staying at Blair Castle in the 19th century, and recorded her thoughts in 'Leaves of a Highland Journal': 'There were several Scottish dishes, two soups and the celebrated haggis, which I tried and really liked very much.'

ABERDEEN, UNION STREET c1900 A90309

STOVED CHICKEN

'Stoved' in the name of this dish derives from the French word 'étouffer' which means to steam by cooking in a covered pot, a relic of the French influence on Scottish cooking that resulted from the 'Auld Alliance' between Scotland and France in the 17th century.

> 1kg/2 lb potatoes, peeled and cut into thin slices
> 2 large onions, peeled and cut into thin slices
> 1 tablespoonful chopped thyme, fresh if possible
> 25g/1oz butter
> 1 tablespoonful cooking oil
> 2 large slices of bacon, de-rinded and chopped into small pieces
> 8 chicken drumsticks or thighs, or a combination of both
> (or 4 large chicken joints, each cut in half)
> 600ml/1 pint chicken stock
> Salt and freshly ground black pepper to taste

Pre-heat the oven to 150°C/300°F/Gas Mark 2. Place a layer of sliced potatoes on the bottom of a large ovenproof casserole. Cover with half the onion slices, and sprinkle with half the chopped thyme, and season to taste.

Heat the butter and oil together in a large frying pan, then brown the chicken pieces on all sides, together with the bacon pieces. Transfer the chicken and bacon to the casserole, reserving the fat in the frying pan. Sprinkle the chicken with the rest of the chopped thyme and season again lightly, then cover the chicken with the remaining sliced onions and then the potato slices, overlapping them neatly on top, and then season again to taste. Pour the chicken stock into the casserole, then brush the reserved fat from the frying pan over the potato slices.

Cover the casserole with a tightly fitting lid, and cook in the pre-heated oven for about 2-2½ hours, until the chicken is really tender. When cooked, remove the lid from the casserole and place the dish under a hot, pre-heated grill for a few minutes, to brown and crisp the potato slices before serving immediately.

RECIPE

CHICKEN IN THE HEATHER

Use Scottish heather honey for this roast chicken dish if possible, for a true flavour of Scotland, but otherwise any clear runny honey can be used.

One roasting chicken, about 1.5kg/3½ lbs in weight
90ml/3 fl oz cooking oil
115g/4fl oz clear heather honey
Salt and freshly ground black pepper
75g/3oz made mustard
Half a teaspoonful curry powder
One clove of garlic, finely chopped

Pre-heat the oven to 190°C/375°F/Gas Mark 4.

Place the chicken in a large ovenproof casserole dish. Mix all the other ingredients together and pour the mixture over the chicken. Cover the dish with its lid and cook in the pre-heated oven for 1 hour.

Baste the chicken thoroughly with the juices and sauce in the dish, then remove the lid and return to the oven to cook, uncovered, for a further 30-40 minutes – this will then brown the chicken.

Serve with boiled or mashed potatoes and fresh seasonal vegetables.

Flavours of ...
SCOTLAND
MEAT, POULTRY & GAME

**STRATHPEFFER, HIGHLAND GIRLS WASHING
THEIR CLOTHES 1890** S421002

25

GROUSE WITH BRANDY AND CREAM SAUCE

Scotland's most famous wild game bird is the grouse. Britain's shooting season officially begins with grouse on 'the glorious 12th' of August. Four varieties of grouse exist in Scotland, Capercaillie, Black Grouse, White Grouse and Red Grouse. The strong, dark meat of Red Grouse is considered by some to be the finest of all game birds. Young birds are best cooked wrapped in bacon rashers and roasted; in the Highlands they are sometimes stuffed with wild raspberries, rowanberries or cranberries, mixed with butter. Older birds are not tender enough for plain roasting, but can be made into a casserole such as in this recipe, which is flavoured with herbs and brandy.

> 4 mature grouse
> 10 button onions (or shallots), peeled but left whole
> 1 stick of celery, trimmed and chopped into pieces
> 225g/8oz mushrooms, trimmed and roughly chopped
> 115g/4oz butter
> About 3 level dessertspoonfuls of plain flour
> 600ml/1 pint stock
> Fresh thyme, marjoram and rosemary, finely chopped
> Salt and black pepper
> 4 tablespoonfuls of double cream
> 2 tablespoonfuls of brandy
> Juice of half a lemon
> 4 slices of white bread, with the crusts removed

Melt half the butter in a flameproof casserole dish. Put the whole onions and the trussed grouse into the pan, and cook in the butter until the grouse are browned on all sides. Take out the grouse and onions and put to one side. Put the celery and mushrooms into the casserole and fry in the remaining butter until soft. Stir in as much flour as is needed to absorb all the fat, and cook gently for a few minutes, stirring occasionally. Gradually blend in the stock, stirring all the time. Increase the heat and continue to stir until the sauce has thickened, then reduce the heat and simmer. Add the herbs and season to taste with salt and pepper. Return the grouse and the onions to the casserole dish, cover with its lid and leave to simmer over a low heat on top of the cooker for about 1½ hours, or until the grouse are tender. Just before serving, mix the cream and brandy together, blend in 3 tablespoonfuls of sauce from the casserole and then stir it all into the casserole dish. Add the lemon juice to sharpen the taste, and adjust the seasoning if necessary. Melt the remaining butter in a frying pan and fry the bread slices on both sides until they are crisp and golden. Drain on kitchen paper, then arrange the slices on a hot serving dish. Place one grouse on each piece of fried bread, pour over a little of the sauce, and sprinkle them with chopped fresh parsley. Serve the rest of the sauce separately.

VENISON CASSEROLE

Many iconic images of Scotland show wild deer roaming the country's mountains, moors and glens. Until the 1700s much of Scotland's population ate wild venison, but after the landowners claimed the Highlands for sheep runs, the poor could usually only obtain this meat by poaching. Nowadays the development of farmed venison has helped revive its popularity, and it is much more readily available to everyone. Venison is a rich and well-flavoured meat, low in cholesterol and high in iron. It can sometimes be dry, but a good way of cooking it is in a pot roast, stew or casserole, to make sure it is tender and juicy.

       1kg/2 lbs 4oz venison braising steak, cut into cubes
       2 tablespoonfuls plain flour, seasoned
       50g/2oz butter
       2 tablespoonfuls oil
       2 onions, peeled and thinly sliced
       1 clove of garlic, peeled and finely chopped
       600ml/1 pint stock
       150ml/ ¼ pint red wine
       1 tablespoonful tomato purée
       225g/8oz carrots
       115g/4oz mushrooms
       2 dessertspoonfuls redcurrant jelly
       Salt and freshly ground black pepper

Pre-heat the oven to 180°C/350°F/Gas Mark 4. Toss the cubes of venison in the seasoned flour so that all sides are covered. Melt half the butter and oil together in a flameproof casserole that has a tight-fitting lid. Fry the venison, a few cubes at a time, until all sides are browned. Put the browned meat to one side and keep warm. Melt the remaining butter and oil in the casserole, add the sliced onions and cook gently for about 10 minutes, until they are soft and transparent, then add the finely chopped garlic. Stir in the remaining seasoned flour and cook for 1-2 minutes, then add the tomato purée, and then the stock and the red wine, a little at a time, stirring continually. Increase the heat and bring the sauce to the boil, constantly stirring as the sauce thickens. Season to taste with salt and pepper, then add the sliced carrots and mushrooms and the browned venison pieces. Put the lid on the casserole and cook in the pre-heated oven for about 1½ - 2 hours. Stir the redcurrant jelly into the casserole 10 minutes before serving. This casserole is even better if it is made the day before needed, and reheated in the oven before serving.

POTATO, ONION AND BACON HOTPOT (OR 'STOVIES')

Potatoes arrived in Britain from the New World in the 16th century, and soon become an everyday food – until then, parsnips formed a major source of carbohydrate in the British diet. Potatoes were most important in the food history of Scotland, since they opened up marginal land for food production and supplemented grain harvests – a contribution of critical importance in areas such as Scotland, where the climate made cereal production so problematical. For cooking purposes, potatoes can be divided into floury or waxy types. Floury potatoes, good for baking, mashing and making chips, are more popular, particularly in Scotland. Farm carts selling 'mealy tatties' – floury potatoes – were a familiar sight in 19th-century Scottish streets. This recipe makes a tasty, filling and cheap supper dish. Either bacon rashers, scraps of cooked bacon leftover from a boiled joint or bacon off-cuts from a butcher can be used. Some grated cheese can also be added to the sauce, if preferred. Do not be too heavy-handed with the salt, as the bacon will make the dish salty anyway. Often known as 'Stovies' in Scotland, this can also be made with leftover cooked meat such as beef and lamb, cut into pieces.

> 4 large potatoes, peeled and cut into thin slices
> 4 large onions, peeled and cut into very thin slices
> 175-225g/6-8oz bacon
> 600ml/1 pint milk
> 50g/2oz plain flour
> 50g/2oz butter or margarine
> Salt and pepper
> 2 tablespoonfuls grated cheese (optional)

Pre-heat the oven to 200°C/400°F/Gas Mark 6. If using bacon rashers, remove the rind, and cut the bacon into small pieces. Grease a casserole with a tight-fitting lid. Fill it with alternating layers of sliced onions, sliced potatoes and bacon pieces, ending with a layer of potatoes. Melt the butter or margarine in a saucepan, stir in the flour and cook gently for 2 minutes. Add the milk, a little at a time, stirring continually so that no lumps are formed. Bring to the boil, stirring constantly until the mixture thickens. (Add the grated cheese now, if using, and stir until it has melted.) Reduce the heat, season to taste, and simmer the sauce for 5 minutes. Pour the white sauce over the bacon and vegetables in the casserole, then give the casserole a good shake to distribute the sauce evenly. Cover the casserole with its lid and bake in the pre-heated oven for 1 hour, then remove the casserole lid, reduce the oven temperature to 150°C/325°F/Gas Mark 4 and bake for a further 1 hour.

LINLITHGOW, AT THE CROSS WELL 1897 39157x

RECIPE

BASHED NEEPS

Bashed Neeps is the traditional accompaniment to haggis, but is also good with meat and sausages. This dish is made with 'brassica rapa', otherwise known as 'rutabaga' or 'Swedish turnip', which is called 'swede' in England. This vegetable was introduced into Scotland in the late 18th century by Patrick Miller of Dalswinton, a director of the Bank of Scotland and also Chairman of the Carron Iron Company. One of Carron's customers, King Gustav III of Sweden, sent Mr Miller a bejewelled snuff-box containing rutabaga seeds, knowing that he had a keen interest in all things agricultural. The snuff-box and the accompanying letter are now in the British Museum.

> 450g/1 lb swede (Swedish turnip),
> peeled and cut into small pieces
> 50g/2oz butter
> Salt and freshly ground black pepper
> A pinch of mace or ground nutmeg (optional)

Cook the swede (Swedish turnip) in boiling water for 25-30 minutes, until it is tender. Drain well.

Add the butter, salt and freshly ground black pepper to taste, and mace or nutmeg if used.

Mash it all together well until the butter is melted and thoroughly mixed in.

RECIPE

RUMBLEDETHUMPS

This wonderfully-named dish is also known as Kailkenny in some parts of Scotland (when cream is used instead of butter). It can either be eaten as a supper dish or as an accompaniment to roast meat or stews. Some versions omit the cheese topping, and others include mashed carrots and turnips.

> 450g/1 lb potatoes, cut into small cubes
> 450g/1 lb cabbage, chopped into small pieces
> 50g/2oz butter or margarine
> 1 large onion, peeled and finely sliced
> Salt and freshly ground black pepper
> 50g/2oz grated hard cheese of choice

Cook the potatoes in boiling water until they are tender. Drain well, then mash. Boil the cabbage until it is tender. Melt the butter in a large saucepan and fry the onion gently until it is soft. Add the mashed potatoes and cabbage, season to taste and mix well.

Pre-heat the oven to 190°C/375°F/Gas Mark 5.

Turn the mixture into a greased shallow ovenproof dish and cover with the grated cheese. Cook in the pre-heated oven for about 20 minutes, until the top is browned.

RECIPE

CLOUTIE DUMPLING

This dish takes its name from the 'clout', or cloth, in which the pudding would have been boiled in the past – sprinkling some flour onto the cloth makes it watertight. The instructions for boiling this in a pudding cloth are given here, and also a modern equivalent, for steaming the pudding in a basin. Cloutie Dumpling is a favourite dish for Christmas time.

BRAEMAR, CLEARING SNOW FROM CAIRNWELL PASS 1879
B266003x

225g/8oz plain flour, sifted
115g/4oz oatmeal
200g/7oz caster sugar
1 teaspoonful ground cinnamon
1 teaspoonful mixed spice
115g/4oz shredded suet
225g/8oz mixed currants and sultanas
115g/4oz stoned dates, finely chopped
1 rounded teaspoonful bicarbonate of soda
1 teaspoonful golden syrup
2 eggs, beaten
250ml/9fl oz milk
A little extra caster sugar, to finish.

Put the flour, oatmeal, sugar, cinnamon, mixed spice, suet, dried fruit and bicarbonate of soda in a bowl. Mix well together, then add the golden syrup, the beaten eggs and as much of the milk as necessary to make a soft but firm batter. Dip a tea towel into a bowl of boiling water, then drain well and lay out flat on a board. Sprinkle the cloth with flour, then a little sugar. Place the dumpling mixture in the middle of the cloth, then tie up the pudding by bringing up the corners of the cloth and securing with string, allowing some room for the dumpling to expand. (Alternatively, use a greased pudding basin, covered with a lid of greased, pleated greaseproof paper, to allow room for expansion, and then another lid of foil, tied down securely with string.) Place a trivet or an upturned saucer in a large saucepan and stand the wrapped pudding (or pudding basin) on top of it. Pour just enough boiling water into the pan to cover the pudding. Cover the pan tightly, bring the water back to the boil then simmer gently for 3-3½ hours. Check the water level from time to time and top up the pan with more boiling water when necessary, so that it does not boil dry. When the cooking time is done, finish the pudding in the oven, as below.

Pre-heat the oven to 180°C/350°F/Gas Mark 4. Remove the pudding carefully from the pan and dip it briefly into a bowl of cold water, to prevent the cloth sticking. Cut the string and remove the cloth, then invert the dumpling onto an ovenproof plate (or turn out from the pudding basin). Bake in the pre-heated oven for 10-15 minutes to finish, or until the skin feels slightly less sticky. Sprinkle with caster sugar and serve at once, with cream or custard.

RECIPE

DUNFILLAN BRAMBLE PUDDING

Wild blackberries, or brambles, grow in many parts of Scotland, although they are less common in the Highlands. They are ripe from early August until late September, and have a much better flavour than the commercially grown blackberries available in supermarkets nowadays – and it's much more fun to go out in the countryside foraging for them. This delicious pudding has a layer of blackberries beneath a sponge topping.

<u>For the fruit layer:</u>
450g/1 lb blackberries
(brambles)
115g/4oz caster sugar
A very small pinch of salt
A pinch of ground cinnamon
(optional)
1 tablespoon water

<u>For the topping:</u>
115g/4oz self-raising flour
50g/2oz butter or margarine,
softened to room temperature
50g/2oz caster sugar
1 egg
A pinch of salt
2 tablespoonfuls milk
Grated zest of 1 lemon

Pre-heat the oven to 180°C/350°F/Gas Mark 4 and butter an ovenproof pie or pudding dish.

Put the blackberries in a heavy-bottomed pan and add one tablespoon of water. Cover the pan with its lid and cook over a gentle heat until the juice begins to run from the berries and they are just soft. Turn the berries and the juice into the prepared pie or pudding dish in layers, sprinkling each layer with sugar. Add the salt and cinnamon, if using, to the final layer.

To make the topping, beat the butter or margarine and sugar together until the mixture is light and fluffy. Beat the egg and gradually mix it in, a little at a time, then beat in the flour, salt, milk and lemon zest. Spread the mixture smoothly over the fruit, and bake in the pre-heated oven for 20-30 minutes, until the sponge topping is risen and golden brown, and firm to the touch.
Serve with cream or custard.

RECIPE

CRANACHAN

This famous recipe is one of Scotland's most delicious desserts, and features the raspberries that Scotland is famous for. The raspberries produced in Scotland are renowned for their flavour, due to their slow ripening in the cool Scottish summers. The main areas of what is regarded by many as Scotland's 'national fruit' are in Tayside, especially the Strathmore valley, but raspberries are also cultivated commercially in Grampian, the Highlands, Arran, the borders and Ayrshire, which is noted for particularly fine fruit. Scotland is also the home of the tayberry, a large conical berry with a bright purple colour and a rich flavour, which was developed at the Scottish Crops Research Institute by crossing a raspberry with a blackberry.

> 50g/2oz medium oatmeal
> 4 tablespoonfuls clear runny honey
> 3 tablespoonfuls whisky
> 300ml/ ½ pint double cream
> 350g/12oz raspberries

Toast the oatmeal in a shallow layer on a sheet of foil under the grill for a few minutes, stirring occasionally, until it is evenly browned but not burnt. Leave to cool. Whip the cream in a large bowl until soft peaks form, then use a large metal spoon to gently fold in the oats, honey and whisky until well combined.

Reserve a few raspberries for decoration, then layer the remainder with the oat mixture in four serving dishes. Cover and chill for 2 hours.

About 30 minutes before serving, transfer the glasses to room temperature. Decorate with the reserved raspberries and serve.

EDINBURGH, THE CASTLE FROM THE GRASSMARKET 1897 39121x

RECIPE

EDINBURGH FOG

This rich and delicious dessert should be served accompanied with fresh fruit such as the raspberries for which Scotland is famous.

> 300ml/ ½ pint cream, double or whipping
> 1 tablespoonful caster sugar
> 1 teaspoonful vanilla sugar (caster sugar in
>   which a vanilla pod has been stored)
> 50g/2oz chopped blanched almonds
> 50g/2oz small ratafia biscuits
> A small amount of sherry for sprinkling

Whisk the cream until it is stiff. Use a large metal spoon to fold in the sugar, vanilla sugar and chopped blanched almonds. Spread out the ratafias on a plate, sprinkle them lightly with the sherry and then stir them very gently into the cream mixture.

Serve the 'fog' in a bowl, with a larger bowl of raspberries set beside it.

GLASGOW, SAUCHIEHALL STREET 1897 39763

Tradition says that Glasgow is where the first tea-room was opened, where women could meet and take refreshment – the coffee-houses which had developed in the 18th and 19th centuries were the haunts of men only. This social development was pioneered by a Miss Kate Cranston, later to be Mrs Cochrane, who in 1884 rented rooms in Aitkin's Hotel in Argyle Street, for her tea-shop. Her business was so successful that she later acquired further premises in Buchanan Street, Ingram Street and 217 Sauchiehall Street – now the Willow Tea Rooms, above Henderson's the Jewellers – in a building designed by Charles Rennie Mackintosh. What could be nicer at teatime than a freshly cooked scone – something that is now enjoyed all over Britain, but which originated from Scotland's wonderful baking tradition. The name 'scone' comes from the Gaelic word 'sgonn', meaning either 'a lump of dough', or 'a large mouthful', and should be pronounced like 'gone', rather than 'cone'.

RECIPE

BUTTERMILK SCONES

This recipe calls for buttermilk, which is rather like runny yoghurt. It can be found in most large supermarkets – look for it in the cream section – and makes these scones very light and soft. If buttermilk proves hard to find, use soured milk, either bought or made at home by stirring 1 teaspoonful of lemon juice into 150ml (¼ pint) of milk, then setting it aside for 1 hour to set. Scones are always best eaten on the day they are made, preferably warm from the oven, and spread with butter and jam.

150ml/ ¼ pint buttermilk (or soured milk if buttermilk
   proves hard to find)
¼ teaspoonful bicarbonate of soda
225g/8oz plain flour
1 level teaspoonful baking powder
A pinch of salt
25g/1oz butter or margarine

Pre-heat the oven to 220°C/425°F/Gas Mark 7. Sift together the flour, baking powder and salt. Rub in the butter or margarine until the mixture resembles fine breadcrumbs. Dissolve the bicarbonate of soda in the buttermilk and stir into the dry ingredients, until you have a soft, elastic white dough. Knead lightly until the dough is smooth and the sides of the bowl are clean. Roll out the dough very gently on a lightly floured surface to about 15mm (¾ inch) thick, or press out the dough with your hands. Use a sharp cutter to stamp out the dough sharply into rounds – do not twist the cutter as you press down, as this affects the rising of the scones. Place the rounds on a greased baking sheet and bake in the pre-heated oven for 10 minutes, then reduce the heat to 200°C/400°F/Gas Mark 6 and cook for a further 5-10 minutes, until the scones are lightly browned.

RECIPE

POTATO SCONES

These scones are very popular in Scotland. They can be eaten either an accompaniment to savoury dishes, such as a bowl of soup, or as a teatime treat, spread with jam.

> 200g/7oz potatoes (use a floury variety),
>   peeled and cut into chunks
> 25g/1oz butter
> 50g/2oz plain flour
> ¼ teaspoonful salt
> ¼ teaspoonful baking powder
> A little cooking oil for brushing the griddle or frying pan

Cook the potatoes in boiling water until tender. Drain thoroughly and return the potatoes to the pan, then add the butter and mash until smooth.

Sift the flour, salt and baking powder into a bowl and add the warm mashed potatoes. Mix it all well together to make a soft dough. With floured hands, shape the dough into two balls, then roll each piece of dough out on a floured board to form two rounds about 5mm (¼ inch) thick. Prick all over the dough with a fork and cut each piece into quarters.

Heat a griddle or heavy-based frying pan to medium-hot, and brush it very lightly with oil. Transfer four quarters of the scone dough to the hot griddle or frying pan and cook them for 3-4 minutes on each side until they are golden brown. Repeat with the remaining quarters. Transfer to a wire rack to cool.

RECIPE

SCOTTISH PANCAKES

These small pancakes are also known as Drop Scones or Pigs' Ears. They are best eaten whilst still warm, spread with butter, and perhaps Scottish honey or jam, if liked.

> 115g/4oz plain flour
> 1 teaspoonful bicarbonate of soda
> 1 teaspoonful cream of tartar
> 25g/1oz butter, cut into small pieces
> 1 egg, beaten
> 150ml/ ¼ pint milk

Lightly grease a griddle (girdle) or a large, heavy-bottomed frying pan, and pre-heat it. Sift the flour, bicarbonate of soda and cream of tartar into a bowl together, then rub in the butter with your fingers until the mixture resembles fine breadcrumbs. Make a well in the centre of the mixture and stir in the beaten egg, together with enough milk to form a thick, creamy batter. Drop spoonfuls of the mixture on to the heated griddle (girdle) or frying pan, spacing them slightly apart.

Cook the pancakes over a steady heat for 2-3 minutes, until bubbles can be seen rising to the surface, then turn them over and cook the other side for a further 2-3 minutes, until the pancakes are golden brown.

Remove the cooked pancakes from the griddle (girdle) or pan and place them inside a folded clean tea towel or napkin on a heated plate to keep warm whilst you cook more pancakes with the remaining mixture – this keeps them soft and moist.

AYR, HIGH STREET 1900 46002

RECIPES

SHORTBREAD

225g/8oz plain flour
115g/4oz caster sugar
115g/4oz semolina or ground rice
225g/8oz butter, cut into small pieces
A little more caster sugar to finish

Pre-heat the oven to 150°C/325°F/Gas Mark 3.

Mix the flour, sugar and semolina or ground rice together in a bowl, then rub in the butter with your fingers until the mixture resembles fine breadcrumbs.

Grease and flour a shallow, round baking tin (18-20cm/7-8 inches in diameter) with butter, or a special shortbread mould if you have one, and press the mixture evenly into it to a thickness of about 2cms (¾ inch). Press around the edge of the dough with your thumb to make a pattern, prick the mixture all over with a fork, and mark it into 6-8 sections.

Alternatively, you can press out the dough on a piece of baking paper until it is a little larger than a 15cm (6 inch) plate, then place the plate on top and cut around it to make a circle of dough. Remove the plate, crimp round the edges of the dough with your finger and thumb, then prick it all over with a fork and mark it into sections, then transfer the dough on the baking paper to a baking sheet.

Bake in the pre-heated oven for about 40 minutes, or until the shortbread is a pale golden colour and just firm to the touch. Leave to cool in the tin, then sprinkle with a little extra caster sugar and cut into sections before serving. Store in an airtight container.

BLACK BUN

Black Bun is traditionally eaten at Christmas and Hogmanay (the Scottish name for New Year's Eve on 31st December), when it is served to visitors with a glass of whisky. Offering food such as Black Bun and shortbread to visitors to the house plays an important part in the Hogmanay celebrations. The first person, or 'first-footer', to cross the threshold of a house after midnight on New Year's Eve should be a propitious one, preferably a tall, dark stranger, and it is the custom to make your Hogmanay visits bearing gifts such as salt, bread, whisky or a lump of coal, to ensure good fortune to the household for the coming year. The first-footer is also supposed to enter the house through the front door, and leave through the back. Black Bun is best made 2-3 months before Christmas and stored, wrapped in foil, in an airtight tin, to allow the flavour to mature.

<u>For the pastry:</u>
450g/1 lb plain flour
¼ teaspoonful salt
225g/8oz butter

<u>For the filling:</u>
350g/12oz self-raising flour
1 teaspoonful cinnamon
1 teaspoonful ground ginger
¼ teaspoonful black pepper
¼ teaspoonful ground nutmeg

450g/1 lb seedless raisins
450g/1 lb currants
50g/2oz mixed peel (optional)
50g/2oz glacé cherries
115g/4oz blanched almonds,
   coarsely chopped
115g/4oz chopped walnuts
2 tablespoonfuls whisky
A small amount of milk
2 egg yolks, beaten

Preheat the oven to 180C/350°F/Gas Mark 4. Mix the flour and salt together and rub in the butter until the mixture resembles fine breadcrumbs. Mix in 1 tablespoonful of cold water, and mix well to form a pastry dough. Grease either a loaf tin or a round cake tin. Set aside a piece of pastry for the lid, then roll out the remainder on a lightly floured surface to about 5mm (¼ inch) thick. Line the loaf or cake tin with the pastry, moulding it against the sides and making sure there are no holes. Mix all the dry ingredients for the filling together and stir well. Add the whisky and stir in, and then enough milk to bring it to a stiff consistency. Fill the tin with the mixture and smooth it off flat at the top. Roll out the pastry lid and lay it on loosely so that the cake mixture can rise a little. Push a long skewer through the lid and filling right to the bottom, in about 8 places. Lightly prick the lid all over with a fork, then brush the lid with the beaten egg yolks. Bake in the pre-heated oven for 2½ - 3 hours until done – test by inserting a skewer into the centre, which should come out clean when the bun is cooked through. Allow the bun to stand in the tin on a wire tray for about 30 minutes before turning out. Serve in slices.

A SHETLAND KNITTER c1890 A001086

RECIPE

BRIDESCAKE

A wedding custom from rural Scotland, and particularly the Orkney and Shetland islands, was associated with 'bridescake' (or bride's bonn, or bun), a small shortbread-like cake flavoured with caraway seeds that was cooked on a griddle (called a girdle in Scotland) by the bride's mother on the wedding day. As the bride entered her new home for the first time, her mother would hold the bridescake over her head, and then break it into pieces; if it broke into a number of small pieces, it was taken as a sign that the marriage would be happy, lucky and fruitful. The broken pieces were then given to the unmarried maidens in the wedding party, who would place them under their pillows so that they might dream about their future husbands – for this reason it was also known as 'dreaming bread'.

> 150g/5oz self-raising flour
> 50g/2oz butter, softened to room temperature
> 25g/1oz caster sugar
> 2 teaspoonfuls of caraway seeds
> 2-3 tablespoonfuls milk, to mix

Sift the flour and rub in the butter. Stir in the caster sugar and caraway seeds, and mix it all to a firm dough, adding a little milk as necessary. Roll out the dough to about 1cm (½ inch) thick, and cut it out into a circle about 18cm (7 inch) in diameter (use a plate to cut around). Lightly score the dough with a knife to mark it into 8 segments, but do not cut right through.

Cook the circle of dough on a pre-heated and greased griddle (or girdle) or heavy frying pan over a medium heat for 8-10 minutes, turning it once, until it is golden brown on both sides. Cool on a wire rack.

RECIPE

SULTANA CAKE

225g/8oz sultanas
115g/4oz butter or margarine
175g/6oz sugar
2 eggs, beaten
A few drops of almond essence
175g/6oz self-raising flour
A pinch of salt

Cover the sultanas with water in a bowl and soak them overnight.
The next day, put the sultanas and water into a saucepan and
bring the water to the boil, then strain the sultanas and whilst
they are still hot mix them with the butter or margarine. Stir in
the sugar, eggs and a few drops of almond essence, then sift in
the flour and salt, and mix it all together well.

Pre-heat the oven to 180°C/350°F/Gas Mark 4. Grease a 20cm (8
inch) round cake tin, and line the bottom of the tin with greased
greaseproof paper. Tip the cake mixture into the prepared tin
and smooth the top. Bake in the pre-heated oven for 30 minutes,
then lower the oven temperature to 150°C/300°F/Gas Mark 2, and
continue to bake until the cake is firm to the touch and a metal
skewer inserted into the centre comes out clean.

RECIPE

DUNDEE MARMALADE TEABREAD

Dundee is known for 'the three Js' – jute, journalism and jam – and the wonderful Dundee Cake, a rich fruit cake that is covered with almonds, but the town has also been famous for Dundee marmalade since a Mr Keiller acquired a cheap batch of particularly bitter Seville oranges from a Spanish ship that had taken refuge from a storm in Dundee's harbour. Mr Keiller was unable to sell the bitter oranges, so his wife, Mrs Janet Keiller, devised a recipe for marmalade to make use of them, which proved popular. Their son James established the Keiller business, and the company soon began to produce jam as well as marmalade, which was enjoyed all over the world. This recipe uses Dundee marmalade to make a teabread to serve cut into slices at teatime.

> 200g/7oz plain flour
> 1 teaspoonful baking powder
> 1 heaped teaspoonful ground cinnamon
> 115g/4 oz butter or margarine, cut into small pieces
> 50g/2oz soft brown sugar
> 4 tablespoonfuls Dundee orange marmalade
> 1 egg, beaten
> 3 tablespoonfuls milk

Pre-heat the oven to 160°C/325°F/Gas Mark 3.

Grease a 1kg (2 lb) loaf tin, and line the base with greased greaseproof paper. Sift the flour, baking powder and cinnamon together into a mixing bowl, add the butter or margarine and rub it in with your fingertips until the mixture resembles fine breadcrumbs, then stir in the sugar. In another bowl, mix together the marmalade, beaten egg and milk, then stir this into the flour and mix thoroughly to make a soft, dropping consistency – add a little more milk if necessary.

Turn the mixture into the prepared loaf tin, and bake in the pre-heated oven for about 1¼ - 1½ hours, until the surface of the cake is firm to the touch. Remove from the oven and leave to cool in the tin for 5 minutes, before turning out onto a wire rack. Peel off the greaseproof paper from the base and leave to cool completely. Serve cut into slices, buttered if liked.

EDINBURGH, JOHN KNOX'S HOUSE 1897 39125

RECIPE

SCOTTISH OATCAKES

Oatmeal became a staple food in Scotland, because the climate and terrain favoured its growth rather than that of other cereals. Oatcakes can be eaten with cheese, or with jam or marmalade for breakfast, or spread with savoury toppings for snacks or canapés. Some Scottish cooks like to use bacon dripping, saved from the breakfast frying pan, instead of butter or margarine to make their oatcakes. Oatcakes can be made cut into rounds and baked in a moderate oven, but true Scottish oatcakes are made in three-sided triangular shapes, known as 'farls', which have been cooked on a girdle, or griddle.

> 225g/8oz fine to medium oatmeal
> ½ teaspoonful of salt
> ¼ teaspoonful bicarbonate of soda
> 25g/1oz butter, margarine or bacon fat, melted
> About 300ml/ ½ pint hot water

Mix the melted fat with the oatmeal, salt and bicarbonate of soda. Add enough hot water to mix all the ingredients into a soft dough. Turn out the dough onto a surface lightly sprinkled with oatmeal and knead it lightly to remove any cracks in the dough, then roll it out very thinly. Rub the dough with a little more oatmeal then cut it into a very large round, then cut the round into triangular segments, or 'farls'.

Grease a girdle (griddle) or a large, heavy frying pan and pre-heat. Carefully slide the oatcakes onto the pre-heated girdle or pan, and cook over a moderate heat until they begin to curl. They should not be turned over, but, if liked, the second side can be toasted under a hot grill until it is crisp, but not brown.

Oatcakes can be served hot after cooking, or transferred to a wire rack to cool and then stored in an airtight container and eaten cold.

RECIPE

INVERNESS GINGERNUTS

225g/8oz plain flour
2 teaspoonfuls ground ginger
1 teaspoonful ground mixed spice
75g/6oz fine oatmeal
75g/3oz caster sugar
Half a teaspoonful bicarbonate of soda
175g/6oz black treacle
75g/3oz butter, cut into small pieces

Pre-heat the oven to 170°C/325°F/Gas Mark 3.

Put the flour, ginger, mixed spice, oatmeal, sugar and bicarbonate of soda into a large bowl, and mix well together. Melt the treacle and butter in a small saucepan over a moderate heat, then pour it onto the dry ingredients and mix it all together well, to form a smooth dough.

Knead the dough well, then roll it out on a lightly floured surface to about 5mm (¼ inch) thick. Prick all over the surface of the dough with a fork, then use a biscuit cutter to stamp out the dough into small rounds about 6cm (2½ inches) in diameter.

Place the biscuit rounds onto greased baking sheets and bake in the pre-heated oven for 20-25 minutes, until they are firm to the touch. Turn out onto a wire tray to cool completely, then store in an airtight container.

RECIPE

PAISLEY ALMOND CAKES

These little cakes are light and fluffy on the inside, and have a delicious crunchy exterior. This amount makes about 12 cakes.

> 50g/2oz cornflour
> 50g/2oz ground rice
> 1 teaspoonful baking powder
> 75g/3oz butter
> 75g/3oz caster sugar
> 40g/1½ oz ground almonds
> 2 eggs, beaten

Pre-heat the oven to 180°C/350°F/Gas Mark 4. Grease 12 patty tins, and line them with paper cases if you wish.

Sieve the cornflour, ground rice and baking powder together into a bowl. In a separate bowl, or in a food mixer, cream the butter and sugar together until it is light and fluffy. Gradually beat in the eggs and the cornflour mixture, alternating between them. When the mixture is white and creamy, lightly stir in the ground almonds.

Half fill the patty tins with the mixture, then bake in the pre-heated oven for 10-15 minutes, until they are risen and golden brown, and firm to the touch. Remove from the oven and leave to cool in the tins for 5 minutes, before turning out on a wire rack to cool completely.

FRANCIS FRITH

PIONEER VICTORIAN PHOTOGRAPHER

Francis Frith, founder of the world-famous photographic archive, was a complex and multi-talented man. A devout Quaker and a highly successful Victorian businessman, he was philosophical by nature and pioneering in outlook. By 1855 he had already established a wholesale grocery business in Liverpool, and sold it for the astonishing sum of £200,000, which is the equivalent today of over £15,000,000. Now in his thirties, and captivated by the new science of photography, Frith set out on a series of pioneering journeys up the Nile and to the Near East.

INTRIGUE AND EXPLORATION

He was the first photographer to venture beyond the sixth cataract of the Nile. Africa was still the mysterious 'Dark Continent', and Stanley and Livingstone's historic meeting was a decade into the future. The conditions for picture taking confound belief. He laboured for hours in his wicker dark-room in the sweltering heat of the desert, while the volatile chemicals fizzed dangerously in their trays. Back in London he exhibited his photographs and was 'rapturously cheered' by members of the Royal Society. His reputation as a photographer was made overnight.

VENTURE OF A LIFE-TIME

By the 1870s the railways had threaded their way across the country, and Bank Holidays and half-day Saturdays had been made obligatory by Act of Parliament. All of a sudden the working man and his family were able to enjoy days out, take holidays, and see a little more of the world.

With typical business acumen, Francis Frith foresaw that these new tourists would enjoy having souvenirs to commemorate their days out. For the next thirty years he travelled the country by train and by pony and trap, producing fine photographs of seaside resorts and beauty spots that were keenly bought by millions of Victorians. These prints were painstakingly pasted into family albums and pored over during the dark nights of winter, rekindling precious memories of summer excursions. Frith's studio was soon supplying retail shops all over the country, and by 1890 F Frith & Co had become the greatest specialist photographic publishing company in the world, with over 2,000 sales outlets, and pioneered the picture postcard.

FRANCIS FRITH'S LEGACY

Francis Frith had died in 1898 at his villa in Cannes, his great project still growing. By 1970 the archive he created contained over a third of a million pictures showing 7,000 British towns and villages.

Frith's legacy to us today is of immense significance and value, for the magnificent archive of evocative photographs he created provides a unique record of change in the cities, towns and villages throughout Britain over a century and more. Frith and his fellow studio photographers revisited locations many times down the years to update their views, compiling for us an enthralling and colourful pageant of British life and character.

We are fortunate that Frith was dedicated to recording the minutiae of everyday life. For it is this sheer wealth of visual data, the painstaking chronicle of changes in dress, transport, street layouts, buildings, housing and landscape that captivates us so much today, offering us a powerful link with the past and with the lives of our ancestors.

Computers have now made it possible for Frith's many thousands of images to be accessed almost instantly. The archive offers every one of us an opportunity to examine the places where we and our families have lived and worked down the years. Its images, depicting our shared past, are now bringing pleasure and enlightenment to millions around the world a century and more after his death.

For further information visit: **www.francisfrith.com**

INTERIOR DECORATION

Frith's photographs can be seen framed and as giant wall murals in thousands of pubs, restaurants, hotels, banks, retail stores and other public buildings throughout Britain. These provide interesting and attractive décor, generating strong local interest and acting as a powerful reminder of gentler days in our increasingly busy and frenetic world.

FRITH PRODUCTS

All Frith photographs are available as prints and posters in a variety of different sizes and styles. In the UK we also offer a range of other gift and stationery products illustrated with Frith photographs, although many of these are not available for delivery outside the UK – see our web site for more information on the products available for delivery in your country.

THE INTERNET

Over 100,000 photographs of Britain can be viewed and purchased on the Frith web site. The web site also includes memories and reminiscences contributed by our customers, who have personal knowledge of localities and of the people and properties depicted in Frith photographs. If you wish to learn more about a specific town or village you may find these reminiscences fascinating to browse. Why not add your own comments if you think they would be of interest to others? See **www.francisfrith.com**

PLEASE HELP US BRING FRITH'S PHOTOGRAPHS TO LIFE

Our authors do their best to recount the history of the places they write about. They give insights into how particular towns and villages developed, they describe the architecture of streets and buildings, and they discuss the lives of famous people who lived there. But however knowledgeable our authors are, the story they tell is necessarily incomplete.

Frith's photographs are so much more than plain historical documents. They are living proofs of the flow of human life down the generations. They show real people at real moments in history; and each of those people is the son or daughter of someone, the brother or sister, aunt or uncle, grandfather or grandmother of someone else. All of them lived, worked and played in the streets depicted in Frith's photographs.

We would be grateful if you would give us your insights into the places shown in our photographs: the streets and buildings, the shops, businesses and industries. Post your memories of life in those streets on the Frith website: what it was like growing up there, who ran the local shop and what shopping was like years ago; if your workplace is shown tell us about your working day and what the building is used for now. Read other visitors' memories and reconnect with your shared local history and heritage. With your help more and more Frith photographs can be brought to life, and vital memories preserved for posterity, and for the benefit of historians in the future.

Wherever possible, we will try to include some of your comments in future editions of our books. Moreover, if you spot errors in dates, titles or other facts, please let us know, because our archive records are not always completely accurate—they rely on 140 years of human endeavour and hand-compiled records. You can email us using the contact form on the website.

Thank you!

For further information, trade, or author enquiries
please contact us at the address below:

**The Francis Frith Collection, 6 Oakley Business Park,
Wylye Road, Dinton, Wiltshire SP3 5EU England.**
Tel: +44 (0)1722 716 376 Fax: +44 (0)1722 716 881
e-mail: sales@francisfrith.co.uk **www.francisfrith.com**